Poems of Power

Ella Wheeler Wilcox

Contents

POEMS OF POWER

BY

Ella Wheeler Wilcox

NOTE

The final word in the title of this volume refers to the DIVINE POWER in every human being, the recognition of which is the secret to all success and happiness. It is this idea which many of the verses endeavour to illustrate.

E. W. W.

THE QUEEN'S LAST RIDE

(Written on the day of Queen Victoria's funeral)

The Queen is taking a drive to-day,
They have hung with purple the carriage-way,
They have dressed with purple the royal track
Where the Queen goes forth and never comes back.

Let no man labour as she goes by
On her last appearance to mortal eye:
With heads uncovered let all men wait
For the Queen to pass, in her regal state.

Army and Navy shall lead the way
For that wonderful coach of the Queen's to-day.
Kings and Princes and Lords of the land
Shall ride behind her, a humble band;
And over the city and over the world
Shall the Flags of all Nations be half-mast-furled,
For the silent lady of royal birth
Who is riding away from the Courts of earth,
Riding away from the world's unrest
To a mystical goal, on a secret quest.

Though in royal splendour she drives through town,
Her robes are simple, she wears no crown:
And yet she wears one, for, widowed no more,
She is crowned with the love that has gone before,
And crowned with the love she has left behind
In the hidden depths of each mourner's mind.

Bow low your heads--lift your hearts on high -
The Queen in silence is driving by!

THE MEETING OF THE CENTURIES

A curious vision on mine eyes unfurled
   In the deep night. I saw, or seemed to see,
   Two Centuries meet, and sit down vis-a-vis
Across the great round table of the world:
One with suggested sorrows in his mien,
   And on his brow the furrowed lines of thought;
   And one whose glad expectant presence brought
A glow and radiance from the realms unseen.

Hand clasped with hand, in silence for a space
   The Centuries sat; the sad old eyes of one
   (As grave paternal eyes regard a son)
Gazing upon that other eager face.
And then a voice, as cadenceless and gray
   As the sea's monody in winter time,
   Mingled with tones melodious, as the chime
Of bird choirs, singing in the dawns of May.

THE OLD CENTURY SPEAKS

By you, Hope stands. With me, Experience walks.
Like a fair jewel in a faded box,
In my tear-rusted heart, sweet Pity lies.
For all the dreams that look forth from your eyes,
And those bright-hued ambitions, which I know
Must fall like leaves and perish, in Time's snow,
(Even as my soul's garden stands bereft,)
I give you pity! 'tis the one gift left.

THE NEW CENTURY

Nay, nay, good friend! not pity, but Godspeed,
Here in the morning of my life I need.
Counsel, and not condolence; smiles, not tears,
To guide me through the channels of the years.
Oh, I am blinded by the blaze of light
That shines upon me from the Infinite.
Blurred is my vision by the close approach
To unseen shores, whereon the times encroach.

THE OLD CENTURY

Illusion, all illusion. List and hear
The Godless cannons, booming far and near.
Flaunting the flag of Unbelief, with Greed
For pilot, lo! the pirate age in speed
Bears on to ruin. War's most hideous crimes
Besmirch the record of these modern times.
Degenerate is the world I leave to you, -

My happiest speech to earth will be--adieu.

THE NEW CENTURY

You speak as one too weary to be just.
I hear the guns--I see the greed and lust.
The death throes of a giant evil fill
The air with riot and confusion. Ill
Ofttimes makes fallow ground for Good; and Wrong
Builds Right's foundation, when it grows too strong.
Pregnant with promise is the hour, and grand
The trust you leave in my all-willing hand.

THE OLD CENTURY

As one who throws a flickering taper's ray
To light departing feet, my shadowed way
You brighten with your faith. Faith makes the man
Alas, that my poor foolish age outran
Its early trust in God! The death of art
And progress follows, when the world's hard heart
Casts out religion. 'Tis the human brain
Men worship now, and heaven, to them, means--gain.

THE NEW CENTURY

Faith is not dead, tho' priest and creed may pass,
For thought has leavened the whole unthinking mass,
And man looks now to find the God within.
We shall talk more of love, and less of sin,
In this new era. We are drawing near
Unatlassed boundaries of a larger sphere.

With awe, I wait, till Science leads us on,
Into the full effulgence of its dawn.

DEATH HAS CROWNED HIM A MARTYR

(Written on the day of President McKinley's death)

In the midst of sunny waters, lo! the mighty Ship of State
Staggers, bruised and torn and wounded by a derelict of fate,
One that drifted from its moorings in the anchorage of hate.

On the deck our noble Pilot, in the glory of his prime,
Lies in woe-impelling silence, dead before his hour or time,
Victim of a mind self-centred in a Godless fool of crime.

One of earth's dissension-breeders, one of Hate's unreasoning tools,
In the annals of the ages, when the world's hot anger cools,
He who sought for Crime's distinction shall be known as Chief of
Fools.

In the annals of the ages, he who had no thought of fame
(Keeping on the path of duty, caring not for praise or blame),
Close beside the deathless Lincoln, writ in light, will shine his
name.

Youth proclaimed him as a hero; time, a statesman; love, a man;
Death has crowned him as a martyr,--so from goal to goal he ran,
Knowing all the sum of glory that a human life may span.

He was chosen by the people; not an accident of birth

Made him ruler of a nation, but his own intrinsic worth.
Fools may govern over kingdoms--not republics of the earth.

He has raised the lovers' standard by his loyalty and faith,
He has shown how virile manhood may keep free from scandal's breath.
He has gazed, with trust unshaken, in the awful eyes of Death.

In the mighty march of progress he has sought to do his best.
Let his enemies be silent, as we lay him down to rest,
And may God assuage the anguish of one suffering woman's breast.

GRIEF

As the funeral train with its honoured dead
    On its mournful way went sweeping,
While a sorrowful nation bowed its head
    And the whole world joined in weeping,
I thought, as I looked on the solemn sight,
    Of the one fond heart despairing,
And I said to myself, as in truth I might,
    "How sad must be this SHARING."

To share the living with even Fame,
    For a heart that is only human,
Is hard, when Glory asserts her claim
    Like a bold, insistent woman;
Yet a great, grand passion can put aside
    Or stay each selfish emotion,
And watch, with a pleasure that springs from pride,
    Its rival--the world's devotion.

But Death should render to love its own,
   And my heart bowed down and sorrowed
For the stricken woman who wept alone
   While even her DEAD was borrowed;
Borrowed from her, the bride--the wife -
   For the world's last martial honour,
As she sat in the gloom of her darkened life,
   With her widow's grief fresh upon her.

He had shed the glory of Love and Fame
   In a golden halo about her;
She had shared his triumphs and worn his name:
   But, alas! he had died without her.
He had wandered in many a distant realm,
   And never had left her behind him,
But now, with a spectral shape at the helm,
   He had sailed where she could not find him.

It was only a thought, that came that day
   In the midst of the muffled drumming
And funeral music and sad display,
   That I knew was right and becoming
Only a thought as the mourning train
   Moved, column after column,
Bearing the dead to the burial plain
   With a reverence grand as solemn.

ILLUSION

God and I in space alone
  And nobody else in view.
"And where are the people, O Lord," I said,
"The earth below, and the sky o'er head,
  And the dead whom once I knew?"

"That was a dream," God smiled and said -
  "A dream that seemed to be true.
There were no people, living or dead,
There was no earth, and no sky o'erhead;
  There was only Myself--in you."

"Why do I feel no fear," I asked,
  "Meeting You here this way?
For I have sinned I know full well?
And is there heaven, and is there hell,
  And is this the judgment day?"

"Say, those were but dreams," the Great God said,
  "Dreams, that have ceased to be.
There are no such things as fear or sin,
There is no you--you never have been -
  There is nothing at all but ME."

ASSERTION

I am serenity. Though passions beat
  Like mighty billows on my helpless heart,
I know beyond them lies the perfect sweet
  Serenity, which patience can impart.
And when wild tempests in my bosom rage,
"Peace, peace," I cry, "it is my heritage."

I am good health. Though fevers rack my brain
  And rude disorders mutilate my strength,
A perfect restoration after pain,
  I know shall be my recompense at length.
And so through grievous day and sleepless night,
"Health, health," I cry, "it is my own by right."

I am success. Though hungry, cold, ill-clad,
  I wander for awhile, I smile and say,
"It is but for a time--I shall be glad
  To-morrow, for good fortune comes my way.
God is my father, He has wealth untold,
His wealth is mine, health, happiness, and gold."

I AM

I know not whence I came,
   I know not whither I go;
But the fact stands clear that I am here
   In this world of pleasure and woe.
And out of the mist and murk
   Another truth shines plain -
It is my power each day and hour
   To add to its joy or its pain.

I know that the earth exists,
   It is none of my business why;
I cannot find out what it's all about,
   I would but waste time to try.
My life is a brief, brief thing,
   I am here for a little space,
And while I stay I would like, if I may,
   To brighten and better the place.

The trouble, I think, with us all
   Is the lack of a high conceit.
If each man thought he was sent to this spot
   To make it a bit more sweet,
How soon we could gladden the world,
   How easily right all wrong,
If nobody shirked, and each one worked
   To help his fellows along!

Cease wondering why you came -
   Stop looking for faults and flaws;

Rise up to-day in your pride and say,
　"I am part of the First Great Cause!
However full the world,
　There is room for an earnest man.
It had need of me, or I would not be -
　I am here to strengthen the plan."

WISHING

Do you wish the world were better?
　Let me tell you what to do:
Set a watch upon your actions,
　Keep them always straight and true;
Rid your mind of selfish motives;
　Let your thoughts be clean and high.
You can make a little Eden
　Of the sphere you occupy.

Do you wish the world were wiser?
　Well, suppose you make a start,
By accumulating wisdom
　In the scrapbook of your heart:
Do not waste one page on folly;
　Live to learn, and learn to live.
If you want to give men knowledge
　You must get it, ere you give.

Do you wish the world were happy?
　Then remember day by day
Just to scatter seeds of kindness

As you pass along the way;
For the pleasures of the many
　　May be ofttimes traced to one,
As the hand that plants an acorn
　　Shelters armies from the sun.

WE TWO

We two make home of any place we go;
We two find joy in any kind of weather;
　　Or if the earth is clothed in bloom or snow,
　　If summer days invite, or bleak winds blow,
What matters it if we two are together?
We two, we two, we make our world, our weather.

We two make banquets of the plainest fare;
In every cup we find the thrill of pleasure;
　　We hide with wreaths the furrowed brow of care,
　　And win to smiles the set lips of despair.
For us life always moves with lilting measure;
We two, we two, we make our world, our pleasure.

We two find youth renewed with every dawn;
Each day holds something of an unknown glory.
　　We waste no thought on grief or pleasure gone;
　　Tricked out like hope, time leads us on and on,
And thrums upon his harp new song or story.
We two, we two, we find the paths of glory.

We two make heaven here on this little earth;
We do not need to wait for realms eternal.
　We know the use of tears, know sorrow's worth,
　And pain for us is always love's rebirth.
Our paths lead closely by the paths supernal;
We two, we two, we live in love eternal.

THE POET'S THEME

What is the explanation of the strange silence of American poets
concerning American triumphs on sea and land?
Literary Digest.

Why should the poet of these pregnant times
Be asked to sing of war's unholy crimes?

To laud and eulogize the trade which thrives
On horrid holocausts of human lives?

Man was a fighting beast when earth was young,
And war the only theme when Homer sung.

'Twixt might and might the equal contest lay,
Not so the battles of our modern day.

Too often now the conquering hero struts
A Gulliver among the Liliputs.

Success no longer rests on skill or fate,
But on the movements of a syndicate.

Of old men fought and deemed it right and just.
To-day the warrior fights because he must,

And in his secret soul feels shame because
He desecrates the higher manhood's laws

Oh! there are worthier themes for poet's pen
In this great hour, than bloody deeds of men

Or triumphs of one hero (though he be
Deserving song for his humility):

The rights of many--not the worth of one;
The coming issues--not the battle done;

The awful opulence, and awful need;
The rise of brotherhood--the fall of greed,

The soul of man replete with God's own force,
The call "to heights," and not the cry "to horse," -

Are there not better themes in this great age
For pen of poet, or for voice of sage

Than those old tales of killing? Song is dumb
Only that greater song in time may come.

When comes the bard, he whom the world waits for,
He will not sing of War.

SONG OF THE SPIRIT

All the aim of life is just
  Getting back to God.
Spirit casting off its dust,
  Getting back to God.
Every grief we have to bear
Disappointment, cross, despair
Each is but another stair
  Climbing back to God.

Step by step and mile by mile -
  Getting back to God;
Nothing else is worth the while -
  Getting back to God.
Light and shadow fill each day
Joys and sorrows pass away,
Smile at all, and smiling, say,
  Getting back to God.

Do not wear a mournful face
  Getting back to God;
Scatter sunshine on the place
  Going back to God;
Take what pleasure you can find,
But where'er your paths may wind.
Keep the purpose well in mind, -
  Getting back to God.

WOMANHOOD

She must be honest, both in thought and deed,
Of generous impulse, and above all greed;
Not seeking praise, or place, or power, or pelf,
But life's best blessings for her higher self,
Which means the best for all.
    She must have faith,
To make good friends of Trouble, Pain, and Death,
And understand their message.
    She should be
As redolent with tender sympathy
As is a rose with fragrance.
    Cheerfulness
Should be her mantle, even though her dress
May be of Sorrow's weaving.
    On her face
A loyal nature leaves its seal of grace,
And chastity is in her atmosphere.
Not that chill chastity which seems austere
(Like untrod snow-peaks, lovely to behold
Till once attained--then barren, loveless, cold);
But the white flame that feeds upon the soul
And lights the pathway to a peaceful goal.
A sense of humour, and a touch of mirth,
To brighten up the shadowy spots of earth;
And pride that passes evil--choosing good.
All these unite in perfect womanhood.

MORNING PRAYER

Let me to-day do something that shall take
  A little sadness from the world's vast store,
And may I be so favoured as to make
  Of joy's too scanty sum a little more
Let me not hurt, by any selfish deed
  Or thoughtless word, the heart of foe or friend;
Nor would I pass, unseeing, worthy need,
  Or sin by silence when I should defend.
However meagre be my worldly wealth,
  Let me give something that shall aid my. kind -
A word of courage, or a thought of health,
  Dropped as I pass for troubled hearts to find.
Let me to-night look back across the span
  'Twixt dawn and dark, and to my conscience say -
Because of some good act to beast or man -
  "The world is better that I lived to-day."

THE VOICES OF THE PEOPLE

Oh! I hear the people calling through the day time and the night
time,
They are calling, they are crying for the coming of the right time.
It behooves you, men and women, it behooves you to be heeding,
For there lurks a note of menace underneath their plaintive
pleading.

Let the land usurpers listen, let the greedy-hearted ponder,
On the meaning of the murmur, rising here and swelling yonder,
Swelling louder, waxing stronger, like a storm-fed stream that
courses
Through the valleys, down abysses, growing, gaining with new forces.

Day by day the river widens, that great river of opinion,
And its torrent beats and plunges at the base of greed's dominion.
Though you dam it by oppression and fling golden bridges o'er it,
Yet the day and hour advances when in fright you'll flee before it.

Yes, I hear the people calling, through the night time and the day
time,
Wretched toilers in life's autumn, weary young ones in life's May
time -
They are crying, they are calling for their share of work and
pleasure;
You are heaping high your coffers while you give them scanty
measure, -
You have stolen God's wide acres, just to glut your swollen purses -
Oh! restore them to His children ere their pleading turns to curses.

THE WORLD GROWS BETTER

Oh! the earth is full of sinning
   And of trouble and of woe,
But the devil makes an inning
   Every time we say it's so.
And the way to set him scowling,
   And to put him back a pace,
Is to stop this stupid growling,
   And to look things in the face.

If you glance at history's pages,
   In all lands and eras known,
You will find the buried ages
   Far more wicked than our own.
As you scan each word and letter.
   You will realise it more,
That the world to-day is better
   Than it ever was before.

There is much that needs amending
   In the present time, no doubt;
There is right that needs amending,
   There is wrong needs crushing out.
And we hear the groans and curses
   Of the poor who starve and die,
While the men with swollen purses
   In the place of hearts go by.

But in spite of all the trouble
  That obscures the sun to-day,
Just remember it was double
  In the ages passed away.
And those wrongs shall all be righted,
  Good shall dominate the land,
For the darkness now is lighted
  By the torch in Science's hand.

Forth from little motes in Chaos,
  We have come to what we are;
And no evil force can stay us -
  We shall mount from star to star,
We shall break each bond and fetter
  That has bound us heretofore;
And the earth is surely better
  Than it ever was before.

A MAN'S IDEAL

A lovely little keeper of the home,
Absorbed in menu books, yet erudite
When I need counsel; quick at repartee
And slow to anger. Modest as a flower,
Yet scintillant and radiant as a star.
Unmercenary in her mould of mind,
While opulent and dainty in her tastes.
A nature generous and free, albeit
The incarnation of economy.
She must be chaste as proud Diana was,

Yet warm as Venus. To all others cold
As some white glacier glittering in the sun;
To me as ardent as the sensuous rose
That yields its sweetness to the burrowing bee
All ignorant of evil in the world,
And innocent as any cloistered nun,
Yet wise as Phryne in the arts of love
When I come thirsting to her nectared lips.
Good as the best, and tempting as the worst,
A saint, a siren, and a paradox.

THE FIRE BRIGADE

Hark! high o'er the rattle and clamour and clatter
  Of traffic-filled streets, do you hear that loud noise?
And pushing and rushing to see what's the matter,
  Like herds of wild cattle, go pell-mell the boys.

There's a fire in the city! the engines are coming!
  The bold bells are clanging, "Make way in the street!"
The wheels of the hose-cart are spinning and humming
  In time to the music of galloping feet.

Make way there! make way there! the horses are flying,
  The sparks from their swift hoofs shoot higher and higher,
The crowds are increasing--the gamins are crying:
  "Hooray, boys!" "Hooray, boys!" "Come on to the fire!"

With clanging and banging and clatter and rattle
  The long ladders follow the engine and hose.

The men are all ready to dash into battle;
  But will they come out again? God only knows.

At windows and doorways crowd questioning faces;
  There's something about it that quickens one's breath.
How proudly the brave fellows sit in their places -
  And speed to the conflict that may be their death!

Still faster and faster and faster and faster
  The grand horses thunder and leap on their way
The red foe is yonder, and may prove the master;
  Turn out there, bold traffic--turn out there, I say!

For once the loud truckman knows oaths will not matter
  And reins in his horses and yields to his fate.
The engines are coming! let pleasure-crowds scatter,
  Let street car and truckman and mail waggon wait.

They speed like a comet--they pass in a minute;
  The boys follow on like a tail to a kite;
The commonplace street has but traffic now in it -
  The great fire engines have swept out of sight.

THE TIDES

Be careful what rubbish you toss in the tide.
  On outgoing billows it drifts from your sight,
But back on the incoming waves it may ride
  And land at your threshold again before night.
Be careful what rubbish you toss in the tide.

Be careful what follies you toss in life's sea.
  On bright dancing billows they drift far away,
But back on the Nemesis tides they may be
  Thrown down at your threshold an unwelcome day
Be careful what follies you toss in youth's sea.

WHEN THE REGIMENT CAME BACK

All the uniforms were blue, all the swords were bright and new,
  When the regiment went marching down the street,
All the men were hale and strong as they proudly moved along,
  Through the cheers that drowned the music of their feet.
Oh the music of the feet keeping time to drums that beat,
  Oh the splendour and the glitter of the sight,
As with swords and rifles new and in uniforms of blue
  The regiment went marching to the fight!

When the regiment came back all the guns and swords were black
  And the uniforms had faded out to gray,
And the faces of the men who marched through that street again

Seemed like faces of the dead who lose their way.
For the dead who lose their way cannot look more wan and gray.
    Oh the sorrow and the pity of the sight,
Oh the weary lagging feet out of step with drums that beat,
    As the regiment comes marching from the fight.

WOMAN TO MAN

Woman is man's enemy, rival, and competitor.--JOHN. J. INGALLS.

You do but jest, sir, and you jest not well,
How could the hand be enemy of the arm,
Or seed and sod be rivals! How could light
Feel jealousy of heat, plant of the leaf,
Or competition dwell 'twixt lip and smile?
Are we not part and parcel of yourselves?
Like strands in one great braid we entertwine
And make the perfect whole. You could not be,
Unless we gave you birth; we are the soil
From which you sprang, yet sterile were that soil
Save as you planted. (Though in the Book we read
One woman bore a child with no man's aid,
We find no record of a man-child born
Without the aid of woman! Fatherhood
Is but a small achievement at the best,
While motherhood comprises heaven and hell.)
This ever-growing argument of sex
Is most unseemly, and devoid of sense.
Why waste more time in controversy, when
There is not time enough for all of love,

Our rightful occupation in this life?
Why prate of our defects, of where we fail,
When just the story of our worth would need
Eternity for telling, and our best
Development comes ever through your praise,
As through our praise you reach your highest self?
Oh! had you not been miser of your praise
And let our virtues be their own reward,
The old-established order of the world
Would never have been changed. Small blame is ours
For this unsexing of ourselves, and worse.
Effeminising of the male. We were
Content, sir, till you starved us, heart and brain.
All we have done, or wise, or otherwise,
Traced to the root, was done for love of you.
Let us taboo all vain comparisons,
And go forth as God meant us, hand in hand,
Companions, mates, and comrades evermore;
Two parts of one divinely ordained whole.

THE TRAVELLER

Reply to Rudyard Kipling's "He travels the fastest who travels alone."

Who travels alone with his eyes on the heights,
Though he laughs in the day time oft weeps in the nights;

For courage goes down at the set of the sun,
When the toil of the journey is all borne by one.

He speeds but to grief though full gaily he ride
Who travels alone without love at his side.

Who travels alone without lover or friend
But hurries from nothing, to naught at the end.

Though great be his winnings and high be his goal,
He is bankrupt in wisdom and beggared in soul.

Life's one gift of value to him is denied
Who travels alone without love at his side.

It is easy enough in this world to make haste
If one live for that purpose--but think of the waste;

For life is a poem to leisurely read,
And the joy of the journey lies not in its speed.

Oh! vain his achievement and petty his pride
Who travels alone without love at his side.

THE EARTH

The earth is yours and mine,
  Our God's bequest.
That testament divine
  Who dare contest?

Usurpers of the earth,
  We claim our share.
We are of royal birth.
  Beware! beware!

Unloose the hand of greed
  From God's fair land,
We claim but what we need -
  That, we demand.

NOW

I leave with God to-morrow's where and how,
And do concern myself but with the Now,
That little word, though half the future's length,
Well used, holds twice its meaning and its strength.

Like one blindfolded groping out his way,
I will not try to touch beyond to-day.
Since all the future is concealed from sight

I need but strive to make the next step right.

That done, the next, and so on, till I find
Perchance some day I am no longer blind,
And looking up, behold a radiant Friend
Who says, "Rest, now, for you have reached the end."

YOU AND TO-DAY

With every rising of the sun
Think of your life as just begun.

The past has shrived and buried deep
All yesterdays--there let them sleep,

Nor seek to summon back one ghost
Of that innumerable host.

Concern yourself with but to-day;
Woo it and teach it to obey

Your wish and will. Since time began
To-day has been the friend of man.

But in his blindness and his sorrow
He looks to yesterday and to-morrow.

You and to-day! a soul sublime
And the great pregnant hour of time.

With God between to bind the train,
Go forth, I say--attain--attain.

THE REASON

Do you know what moves the tides
  As they swing from low to high?
'Tis the love, love, love,
  Of the moon within the sky.
Oh! they follow where she guides,
Do the faithful-hearted tides.

Do you know what moves the earth
  Out of winter into spring?
'Tis the love, love, love,
  Of the sun, the mighty king.
Oh the rapture that finds birth
In the kiss of sun and earth!

Do you know what makes sweet songs
  Ring for me above earth's strife?
'Tis the love, love, love,
  That you bring into my life,
Oh the glory of the songs
In the heart where love belongs!

MISSION

If you are sighing for a lofty work,
  If great ambitions dominate your mind,
Just watch yourself and see you do not shirk
  The common little ways of being kind.

If you are dreaming of a future goal,
  When, crowned with glory, men shall own your power,
Be careful that you let no struggling soul
  Go by unaided in the present hour.

If you are moved to pity for the earth,
  And long to aid it, do not look so high,
You pass some poor, dumb creature faint with thirst -
  All life is equal in the eternal eye.

If you would help to make the wrong things right,
  Begin at home: there lies a lifetime's toil.
Weed your own garden fair for all men's sight,
  Before you plan to till another's soil.

God chooses His own leaders in the world,
  And from the rest He asks but willing hands.
As mighty mountains into place are hurled,
  While patient tides may only shape the sands.

REPETITION

Over and over and over
  These truths I will weave in song -
That God's great plan needs you and me,
That will is greater than destiny,
  And that love moves the world along.

However mankind may doubt it,
  It shall listen and hear my creed -
That God may ever be found within,
That the worship of self is the only sin,
  And the only devil is greed.

Over and over and over
  These truths I will say and sing,
That love is mightier far than hate,
That a man's own thought is a man's own fate,
  And that life is a goodly thing.

BEGIN THE DAY

Begin each morning with a talk to God,
And ask for your divine inheritance
Of usefulness, contentment, and success.
Resign all fear, all doubt, and all despair.
The stars doubt not, and they are undismayed,

Though whirled through space for countless centuries,
And told not why or wherefore: and the sea
With everlasting ebb and flow obeys,
And leaves the purpose with the unseen Cause.
The star sheds radiance on a million worlds,
The sea is prodigal with waves, and yet
No lustre from the star is lost, and not
One drop is missing from the ocean tides.
Oh! brother to the star and sea, know all
God's opulence is held in trust for those
Who wait serenely and who work in faith.

WORDS

Words are great forces in the realm of life:
   Be careful of their use. Who talks of hate,
Of poverty, of sickness, but sets rife
   These very elements to mar his fate.

When love, health, happiness, and plenty hear
   Their names repeated over day by day,
They wing their way like answering fairies near,
   Then nestle down within our homes to stay.

Who talks of evil conjures into shape
   The formless thing and gives it life and scope.
This is the law: then let no word escape
   That does not breathe of everlasting hope.

FATE AND I

Wise men tell me thou, O Fate,
Art invincible and great.

Well, I own thy prowess; still
Dare I flout thee with my will

Thou canst shatter in a span
All the earthly pride of man.

Outward things thou canst control;
But stand back--I rule my soul!

Death? 'Tis such a little thing -
Scarcely worth the mentioning.

What has death to do with me,
Save to set my spirit free?

Something in me dwells, O Fate,
That can rise and dominate

Loss, and sorrow, and disaster, -
How, then, Fate, art thou my master?

In the great primeval morn
My immortal will was born,

Part of that stupendous Cause
Which conceived the Solar Laws,

Lit the suns and filled the seas,
Royalest of pedigrees.

That great Cause was Love, the Source
Who most loves has most of Force.

He who harbours Hate one hour
Saps the soul of Peace and Power.

He who will not hate his foe
Need not dread life's hardest blow.

In the realm of brotherhood
Wishing no man aught but good,

Naught but good can come to me -
This is Love's supreme decree.

Since I bar my door to Hate,
What have I to fear, O Fate?

Since I fear not--Fate I vow,
I the ruler am, not thou!

ATTAINMENT

Use all your hidden forces. Do not miss
The purpose of this life, and do not wait
For circumstance to mould or change your fate;
In your own self lies Destiny. Let this
Vast truth cast out all fear, all prejudice,
All hesitation. Know that you are great,
Great with divinity. So dominate
Environment, and enter into bliss.
Love largely and hate nothing. Hold no aim
That does not chord with universal good.
Hear what the voices of the Silence say -
All joys are yours if you put forth your claim.
Once let the spiritual laws be understood,
Material things must answer and obey.

A PLEA TO PEACE

When mighty issues loom before us, all
The petty great men of the day seem small,
Like pigmies standing in a blaze of light
Before some grim majestic mountain-height.
War, with its bloody and impartial hand,
Reveals the hidden weakness of a land,
Uncrowns the heroes trusting Peace has made
Of men whose honour is a thing of trade,

And turns the searchlight full on many a place
Where proud conventions long have masked disgrace.
O lovely Peace! as thou art fair be wise.
Demand great men, and great men shall arise
To do thy bidding. Even as warriors come,
Swift at the call of bugle and of drum,
So at the voice of Peace, imperative
As bugle's call, shall heroes spring to live
For country and for thee. In every land,
In every age, men are what times demand.
Demand the best, O Peace, and teach thy sons
They need not rush in front of death-charged guns
With murder in their hearts to prove their worth.
The grandest heroes who have graced the earth
Were love-filled souls who did not seek the fray,
But chose the safe, hard, high, and lonely way
Of selfless labour for a suffering world.
Beneath our glorious flag again unfurled
In victory such heroes wait to be
Called into bloodless action, Peace, by thee.
Be thou insistent in thy stern demand,
And wise, great men shall rise up in the land.

PRESUMPTION

Whenever I am prone to doubt or wonder -
  I check myself, and say, "That mighty One
Who made the solar system cannot blunder -
  And for the best all things are being done."
Who set the stars on their eternal courses

Has fashioned this strange earth by some sure plan.
Bow low, bow low to those majestic forces,
　Nor dare to doubt their wisdom, puny man.

You cannot put one little star in motion,
　You cannot shape one single forest leaf,
Nor fling a mountain up, nor sink an ocean,
　Presumptuous pigmy, large with unbelief.
You cannot bring one dawn of regal splendour,
　Nor bid the day to shadowy twilight fall,
Nor send the pale moon forth with radiance tender -
　And dare you doubt the One who has done all?

"So much is wrong, there is such pain--such sinning."
　Yet look again--behold how much is right!
And He who formed the world from its beginning
　Knows how to guide it upward to the light.
Your task, O man, is not to carp and cavil
　At God's achievements, but with purpose strong
To cling to good, and turn away from evil.
　That is the way to help the world along.

HIGH NOON

Time's finger on the dial of my life
Points to high noon! and yet the half-spent day
Leaves less than half remaining, for the dark,
Bleak shadows of the grave engulf the end.
To those who burn the candle to the stick,
The sputtering socket yields but little light.
Long life is sadder than an early death.
We cannot count on ravelled threads of age
Whereof to weave a fabric. We must use
The warp and woof the ready present yields
And toil while daylight lasts. When I bethink
How brief the past, the future, still more brief
Calls on to action, action! Not for me
Is time for retrospection or for dreams,
Not time for self-laudation or remorse.
Have I done nobly? Then I must not let
Dead yesterday unborn to-morrow shame.
Have I done wrong? Well, let the bitter taste
Of fruit that turned to ashes on my lip
Be my reminder in temptation's hour,
And keep me silent when I would condemn.
Sometimes it takes the acid of a sin
To cleanse the clouded windows of our souls
So pity may shine through them.

    Looking back,
My faults and errors seem like stepping-stones
That led the way to knowledge of the truth
And made me value virtue; sorrows shine

In rainbow colours o'er the gulf of years,
Where lie forgotten pleasures.

    Looking forth,
Out to the western sky still bright with noon,
I feel well spurred and booted for the strife
That ends not till Nirvana is attained.

Battling with fate, with men, and with myself,
Up the steep summit of my life's forenoon,
Three things I learned, three things of precious worth,
To guide and help me down the western slope.
I have learned how to pray, and toil, and save:
To pray for courage to receive what comes,
Knowing what comes to be divinely sent;
To toil for universal good, since thus
And only thus can good come unto me;
To save, by giving whatsoe'er I have
To those who have not--this alone is gain.

THOUGHT-MAGNETS

With each strong thought, with every earnest longing
    For aught thou deemest needful to thy soul,
Invisible vast forces are set thronging
    Between thee and that goal

'Tis only when some hidden weakness alters
    And changes thy desire, or makes it less,
That this mysterious army ever falters
    Or stops short of success.

Thought is a magnet; and the longed-for pleasure,
   Or boon, or aim, or object, is the steel;
And its attainment hangs but on the measure
   Of what thy soul can feel.

SMILES

Smile a little, smile a little,
   As you go along,
Not alone when life is pleasant,
   But when things go wrong.
Care delights to see you frowning,
   Loves to hear you sigh;
Turn a smiling face upon her -
   Quick the dame will fly.

Smile a little, smile a little,
   All along the road;
Every life must have its burden,
   Every heart its load.
Why sit down in gloom and darkness
   With your grief to sup?
As you drink Fate's bitter tonic,
   Smile across the cup.

Smile upon the troubled pilgrims
   Whom you pass and meet;
Frowns are thorns, and smiles are blossoms
   Oft for weary feet.
Do not make the way seem harder

By a sullen face;
Smile a little, smile a little,
  Brighten up the place.

Smile upon your undone labour;
  Not for one who grieves
O'er his task waits wealth or glory;
  He who smiles achieves.
Though you meet with loss and sorrow
  In the passing years,
Smile a little, smile a little,
  Even through your tears.

THE UNDISCOVERED COUNTRY

Man has explored all countries and all lands,
And made his own the secrets of each clime.
Now, ere the world has fully reached its prime,
The oval earth lies compassed with steel bands,
The seas are slaves to ships that touch all strands,
  And even the haughty elements, sublime
  And bold, yield him their secrets for all time,
And speed like lackeys forth at his commands.

Still, though he search from shore to distant shore,
  And no strange realms, no unlocated plains
Are left for his attainment and control,
Yet is there one more kingdom to explore.
  Go, know thyself, O man! there yet remains
The undiscovered country of thy soul!

THE UNIVERSAL ROUTE

As we journey along, with a laugh and a song,
  We see, on youth's flower-decked slope,
Like a beacon of light, shining fair on the sight,
  The beautiful Station of Hope.

But the wheels of old Time roll along as we climb,
  And our youth speeds away on the years;
And with hearts that are numb with life's sorrows we come
  To the mist-covered Station of Tears.

Still onward we pass, where the milestones, alas!
  Are the tombs of our dead, to the West,
Where glitters and gleams, in the dying sunbeams,
  The sweet, silent Station of Rest.

All rest is but change, and no grave can estrange
  The soul from its Parent above;
And, scorning the rod, it soars back to its God,
  To the limitless City of Love.

UNANSWERED PRAYERS

Like some schoolmaster, kind in being stern,
Who hears the children crying o'er their slates
And calling, "Help me, master!" yet helps not,
Since in his silence and refusal lies
Their self-development, so God abides
Unheeding many prayers. He is not deaf
To any cry sent up from earnest hearts;
He hears and strengthens when He must deny.
He sees us weeping over life's hard sums;
But should He give the key and dry our tears,
What would it profit us when school were done
And not one lesson mastered?

　　What a world
Were this if all our prayers were answered. Not
In famed Pandora's box were such vast ills
As lie in human hearts. Should our desires,
Voiced one by one in prayer, ascend to God
And come back as events shaped to our wish,
What chaos would result!

　　In my fierce youth
I sighed out breath enough to move a fleet,
Voicing wild prayers to heaven for fancied boons
Which were denied; and that denial bends
My knee to prayers of gratitude each day
Of my maturer years. Yet from those prayers
I rose alway regirded for the strife
And conscious of new strength. Pray on, sad heart,

That which thou pleadest for may not be given,
But in the lofty altitude where souls
Who supplicate God's grace are lifted, there
Thou shalt find help to bear thy daily lot
Which is not elsewhere found.

THANKSGIVING

We walk on starry fields of white
  And do not see the daisies,
For blessings common in our sight
  We rarely offer praises.
We sigh for some supreme delight
  To crown our lives with splendour,
And quite ignore our daily store
  Of pleasures sweet and tender.

Our cares are bold and push their way
  Upon our thought and feeling;
They hang about us all the day,
  Our time from pleasure stealing.
So unobtrusive many a joy
  We pass by and forget it,
But worry strives to own our lives,
  And conquers if we let it.

There's not a day in all the year
  But holds some hidden pleasure,
And, looking back, joys oft appear
  To brim the past's wide measure.

But blessings are like friends, I hold,
  Who love and labour near us.
We ought to raise our notes of praise
  While living hearts can hear us.

Full many a blessing wears the guise
  Of worry or of trouble;
Far-seeing is the soul, and wise,
  Who knows the mask is double.
But he who has the faith and strength
  To thank his God for sorrow
Has found a joy without alloy
  To gladden every morrow.

We ought to make the moments notes
  Of happy, glad Thanksgiving;
The hours and days a silent phrase
  Of music we are living.
And so the theme should swell and grow
  As weeks and months pass o'er us,
And rise sublime at this good time,
  A grand Thanksgiving chorus.

CONTRASTS

I see the tall church steeples -
  They reach so far, so far;
But the eyes of my heart see the world's great mart
Where the starving people are.

I hear the church bells ringing
   Their chimes on the morning air;
But my soul's sad ear is hurt to hear
   The poor man's cry of despair.

Thicker and thicker the churches,
   Nearer and nearer the sky -
But alack for their creeds while the poor man's needs
   Grow deeper as years roll by!

THY SHIP

Hadst thou a ship, in whose vast hold lay stored
The priceless riches of all climes and lands,
Say, wouldst thou let it float upon the seas
Unpiloted, of fickle winds the sport,
And of wild waves and hidden rocks the prey?

Thine is that ship; and in its depths concealed
Lies all the wealth of this vast universe -
Yea, lies some part of God's omnipotence,
The legacy divine of every soul.
Thy will, O man, thy will is that great ship,
And yet behold it drifting here and there -
One moment lying motionless in port,
Then on high seas by sudden impulse flung,
Then drying on the sands, and yet again
Sent forth on idle quests to no-man's land
To carry nothing and to nothing bring;
Till, worn and fretted by the aimless strife

And buffeted by vacillating winds,
It founders on a rock, or springs a leak,
With all its unused treasures in the hold.

Go save thy ship, thou sluggard; take the wheel
And steer to knowledge, glory, and success.
Great mariners have made the pathway plain
For thee to follow; hold thou to the course
Of Concentration Channel, and all things
Shall come in answer to thy swerveless wish
As comes the needle to the magnet's call,
Or sunlight to the prisoned blade of grass
That yearns all winter for the kiss of spring.

LIFE

All in the dark we grope along,
   And if we go amiss
We learn at least which path is wrong,
   And there is gain in this.

We do not always win the race
   By only running right;
We have to tread the mountain's base
   Before we reach its height.

The Christs alone no errors made;
   So often had they trod
The paths that lead through light and shade,
   They had become as God.

As Krishna, Buddha, Christ again,
　They passed along the way,
And left those mighty truths which men
　But dimly grasp to-day.

But he who loves himself the last
　And knows the use of pain,
Though strewn with errors all his past,
　He surely shall attain.

Some souls there are that needs must taste
　Of wrong, ere choosing right;
We should not call those years a waste
　Which led us to the light.

A MARINE ETCHING

A yacht from its harbour ropes pulled free,
And leaped like a steed o'er the race-track blue,
Then up behind her the dust of the sea,
A gray fog, drifted, and hid her from view.

"LOVE THYSELF LAST"

Love thyself last. Look near, behold thy duty
  To those who walk beside thee down life's road.
Make glad their days by little acts of beauty
  And help them bear the burden of earth's load.

Love thyself last. Look far and find the stranger
  Who staggers 'neath his sin and his despair;
Go, lend a hand, and lead him out of danger,
  To heights where he may see the world is fair.

Love thyself last. The vastnesses above thee
  Are filled with Spirit-Forces; strong and pure
And fervently these faithful friends shall love thee
  Keep thou thy watch o'er others and endure.

Love thyself last, and oh! such joy shall thrill thee
  As never yet to selfish souls was given;
Whate'er thy lot, a perfect peace will fill thee,
  And earth shall seem the ante-room of Heaven.

Love thyself last, and thou shalt grow in spirit
  To see, to hear, to know, and understand.
The message of the stars, lo, thou shalt hear it,
  And all God's joys shall be at thy command.

CHRISTMAS FANCIES

When Christmas bells are swinging above the fields of snow,
We hear sweet voices ringing from lands of long ago,
  And etched on vacant places
  Are half-forgotten faces
Of friends we used to cherish, and loves we used to know -
When Christmas bells are swinging above the fields of snow.

Uprising from the ocean of the present surging near,
We see, with strange emotion, that is not free from fear,
  That continent Elysian
  Long vanished from our vision,
Youth's lovely lost Atlantis, so mourned for and so dear,
Uprising from the ocean of the present surging near.

When gloomy, gray Decembers are roused to Christmas mirth,
The dullest life remembers there once was joy on earth,
  And draws from youth's recesses
  Some memory it possesses,
And, gazing through the lens of time, exaggerates its worth,
When gloomy, gray December is roused to Christmas mirth.

When hanging up the holly or mistletoe, I wis
Each heart recalls some folly that lit the world with bliss.
  Not all the seers and sages
  With wisdom of the ages
Can give the mind such pleasure as memories of that kiss
When hanging up the holly or mistletoe, I wis.

For life was made for loving, and love alone repays,

As passing years are proving, for all of Time's sad ways.
   There lies a sting in pleasure,
   And fame gives shallow measure,
And wealth is but a phantom that mocks the restless days,
For life was made for loving, and only loving pays.

When Christmas bells are pelting the air with silver chimes,
And silences are melting to soft, melodious rhymes,
   Let Love, the world's beginning,
   End fear and hate and sinning;
Let Love, the God Eternal, be worshipped in all climes
When Christmas bells are pelting the air with silver chimes.

THE RIVER

I am a river flowing from God's sea
Through devious ways. He mapped my course for me;
I cannot change it; mine alone the toil
To keep the waters free from grime and soil.
The winding river ends where it began;
And when my life has compassed its brief span
I must return to that mysterious source.
So let me gather daily on my course
The perfume from the blossoms as I pass,
Balm from the pines, and healing from the grass,
And carry down my current as I go
Not common stones but precious gems to show;
And tears (the holy water from sad eyes)
Back to God's sea, from which all rivers rise,
Let me convey, not blood from wounded hearts,

Nor poison which the upas tree imparts.
When over flowery vales I leap with joy,
Let me not devastate them, nor destroy,
But rather leave them fairer to the sight;
Mine be the lot to comfort and delight.
And if down awful chasms I needs must leap,
Let me not murmur at my lot, but sweep
On bravely to the end without one fear,
Knowing that He who planned my ways stands near.
Love sent me forth, to Love I go again,
For Love is all, and over all. Amen.

SORRY

There is much that makes me sorry as I journey down life's way,
And I seem to see more pathos in poor human lives each day.
I'm sorry for the strong, brave men who shield the weak from harm,
But who, in their own troubled hours, find no protecting arm.

I'm sorry for the victors who have reached success, to stand
As targets for the arrows shot by envious failure's hand.
I'm sorry for the generous hearts who freely shared their wine,
But drink alone the gall of tears in fortune's drear decline.

I'm sorry for the souls who build their own fame's funeral pyre,
Derided by the scornful throng like ice deriding fire.
I'm sorry for the conquering ones who know not sin's defeat,
But daily tread down fierce desire 'neath scorched and bleeding feet.

I'm sorry for the anguished hearts that break with passion's strain,
But I'm sorrier for the poor starved souls that never knew love's
pain,
Who hunger on through barren years not tasting joys they crave,
For sadder far is such a lot than weeping o'er a grave.

I'm sorry for the souls that come unwelcomed into birth,
I'm sorry for the unloved old who cumber up the earth,
I'm sorry for the suffering poor in life's great maelstrom hurled -
In truth, I'm sorry for them all who make this aching world.

But underneath whate'er seems sad and is not understood,
I know there lies hid from our sight a mighty germ of good.
And this belief stands firm by me, my sermon, motto, text -
The sorriest things in this life will seem grandest in the next.

AMBITION'S TRAIL

If all the end of this continuous striving
    Were simply TO ATTAIN,
How poor would seem the planning and contriving,
The endless urging and the hurried driving,
    Of body, heart, and brain!

But ever in the wake of true achieving
    There shines this glowing trail -
Some other soul will be spurred on, conceiving
New strength and hope, in its own power believing,
    Because THOU didst not fail.

Not thine alone the glory, nor the sorrow,
    If thou dost miss the goal;
Undreamed of lives in many a far to-morrow
From thee their weakness or their force shall borrow -
    On, on, ambitious soul.

UNCONTROLLED

The mighty forces of mysterious space
    Are one by one subdued by lordly man.
    The awful lightning that for eons ran
    Their devastating and untrammelled race,
Now bear his messages from place to place
    Like carrier doves. The winds lead on his van;
    The lawless elements no longer can
Resist his strength, but yield with sullen grace.

His bold feet scaling heights before untrod,
    Light, darkness, air and water, heat and cold,
        He bids go forth and bring him power and pelf.
And yet, though ruler, king and demi-god,
    He walks with his fierce passions uncontrolled,
        The conqueror of all things--save himself.

WILL

You will be what you will to be;
   Let failure find its false content
   In that poor word "environment,"
But spirit scorns it, and is free.

It masters time, it conquers space,
   It cowes that boastful trickster Chance,
   And bids the tyrant Circumstance
Uncrown and fill a servant's place.

The human Will, that force unseen,
   The offspring of a deathless Soul,
   Can hew the way to any goal,
Though walls of granite intervene.

Be not impatient in delay,
   But wait as one who understands;
   When spirit rises and commands,
The gods are ready to obey.

The river seeking for the sea
   Confronts the dam and precipice,
   Yet knows it cannot fail or miss;
YOU WILL BE WHAT YOU WILL TO BE!

TO AN ASTROLOGER

Nay, seer, I do not doubt thy mystic lore,
Nor question that the tenor of my life,
Past, present, and the future, is revealed
There in my horoscope. I do believe
That yon dead moon compels the haughty seas
To ebb and flow, and that my natal star
Stands like a stern-browed sentinel in space
And challenges events; nor lets one grief,
Or joy, or failure, or success, pass on
To mar or bless my earthly lot, until
It proves its Karmic right to come to me.

All this I grant, but more than this I KNOW!
Before the solar systems were conceived,
When nothing was but the unnamable,
My spirit lived, an atom of the Cause.
Through countless ages and in many forms
It has existed, ere it entered in
This human frame to serve its little day
Upon the earth. The deathless Me of me.
The spark from that great all-creative fire,
Is part of that eternal source called God,
And mightier than the universe.

        Why, he
Who knows, and knowing, never once forgets
The pedigree divine of his own soul,
Can conquer, shape, and govern destiny,
And use vast space as 'twere a board for chess

With stars for pawns; can change his horoscope
To suit his will; turn failure to success,
And from preordained sorrows, harvest joy.

There is no puny planet, sun, or moon,
Or zodiacal sign which can control
The God in us! If we bring THAT to bear
Upon events, we mould them to our wish;
'Tis when the infinite 'neath the finite gropes
That men are governed by their horoscopes.

THE TENDRIL'S FATE

Under the snow, in the dark and the cold,
  A pale little sprout was humming;
Sweetly it sang, 'neath the frozen mould,
  Of the beautiful days that were coming.

"How foolish your songs!" said a lump of clay;
  "What is there, I ask, to prove them?
Just look at the walls between you and the day,
  Now, have you the strength to move them?"

But under the ice and under the snow
  The pale little sprout kept singing,
"I cannot tell how, but I know, I know,
  I know what the days are bringing.

"Birds, and blossoms, and buzzing bees,
  Blue, blue skies above me,

Bloom on the meadows and buds on the trees
    And the great glad sun to love me."

A pebble spoke next: "You are quite absurd,"
    It said, "with your song's insistence;
For *I* never saw a tree or a bird,
    So of course there are none in existence."

"But I know, I know," the tendril cried,
    In beautiful sweet unreason;
Till lo! from its prison, glorified,
    It burst in the glad spring season.

THE TIMES

The times are not degenerate. Man's faith
Mounts higher than of old. No crumbling creed
Can take from the immortal soul the need
    Of that supreme Creator, God. The wraith
Of dead beliefs we cherished in our youth
Fades but to let us welcome new-born Truth.

Man may not worship at the ancient shrine
Prone on his face, in self-accusing scorn.
That night is past. He hails a fairer morn,
    And knows himself a something all divine;
Not humble worm whose heritage is sin,
But, born of God, he feels the Christ withal.

Not loud his prayers, as in the olden time,

But deep his reverence for that mighty force,
That occult working of the great All-Source,
  Which makes the present era so sublime.
Religion now means something high and broad.
And man stood never half so near to God.

THE QUESTION

Beside us in our seeking after pleasures,
  Through all our restless striving after fame,
Through all our search for worldly gains and treasures,
  There walketh one whom no man likes to name.
Silent he follows, veiled of form and feature,
  Indifferent if we sorrow or rejoice,
Yet that day comes when every living creature
  Must look upon his face and hear his voice.

When that day comes to you, and Death, unmasking,
  Shall bar your path, and say, "Behold the end,"
What are the questions that he will be asking
  About your past? Have you considered, friend?
I think he will not chide you for your sinning,
  Nor for your creeds or dogmas will he care;
He will but ask, "From your life's first beginning
  How many burdens have you helped to bear?"

SORROW'S USES

The uses of sorrow I comprehend
Better and better at each year's end.

Deeper and deeper I seem to see
Why and wherefore it has to be.

Only after the dark, wet days
Do we fully rejoice in the sun's bright rays.

Sweeter the crust tastes after the fast
Than the sated gourmand's finest repast.

The faintest cheer sounds never amiss
To the actor who once has heard a hiss.

To one who the sadness of freedom knows,
Light seem the fetters love may impose.

And he who has dwelt with his heart alone,
Hears all the music in friendship's tone.

So better and better I comprehend
How sorrow ever would be our friend.

IF

'Twixt what thou art, and what thou wouldst be, let
No "If" arise on which to lay the blame.
Man makes a mountain of that puny word,
But, like a blade of grass before the scythe,
It falls and withers when a human will,
Stirred by creative force, sweeps toward its aim.

Thou wilt be what thou couldst be. Circumstance
Is but the toy of genius. When a soul
Burns with a god-like purpose to achieve,
All obstacles between it and its goal
Must vanish as the dew before the sun.

"If" is the motto of the dilettante
And idle dreamer; 'tis the poor excuse
Of mediocrity. The truly great
Know not the word, or know it but to scorn,
Else had Joan of Arc a peasant died,
Uncrowned by glory and by men unsung.

WHICH ARE YOU?

There are two kinds of people on earth to-day;
Just two kinds of people, no more, I say.

Not the sinner and saint, for it's well understood
The good are half bad, and the bad are half good.

Not the rich and the poor, for to rate a man's wealth
You must first know the state of his conscience and health.

Not the humble and proud, for, in life's little span,
Who puts on vain airs is not counted a man.

Not the happy and sad, for the swift flying years
Bring each man his laughter, and each man his tears.

No; the two kinds of people on earth I mean
Are the people who lift, and the people who lean.

Wherever you go, you will find the earth's masses
Are always divided in just these two classes.

And, oddly enough, you will find too, I ween,
There's only one lifter to twenty who lean.

In which class are you? Are you easing the load
Of overtaxed lifters, who toil down the road?

Or are you a leaner, who lets others share
Your portion of labour and worry and care?

THE CREED TO BE

Our thoughts are moulding unmade spheres,
    And, like a blessing or a curse,
They thunder down the formless years,
    And ring throughout the universe.

We build our futures by the shape
    Of our desires, and not by acts.
There is no pathway of escape;
    No priest-made creeds can alter facts.

Salvation is not begged or bought;
    Too long this selfish hope sufficed;
Too long man reeked with lawless thought,
    And leaned upon a tortured Christ.

Like shrivelled leaves, these worn-out creeds
    Are dropping from Religion's tree;
The world begins to know its needs,
    And souls are crying to be free.

Free from the load of fear and grief,
    Man fashioned in an ignorant age;
Free from the ache of unbelief
    He fled to in rebellious rage.

No church can bind him to the things
    That fed the first crude souls, evolved;
For, mounting up on daring wings,
    He questions mysteries all unsolved.

Above the chant of priests, above
   The blatant voice of braying doubt,
He hears the still, small voice of Love,
   Which sends its simple message out.

And clearer, sweeter, day by day,
   Its mandate echoes from the skies,
"Go roll the stone of self away,
   And let the Christ within thee rise."

INSPIRATION

Not like a daring, bold, aggressive boy,
   Is inspiration, eager to pursue,
But rather like a maiden, fond, yet coy,
   Who gives herself to him who best doth woo.

Once she may smile, or thrice, thy soul to fire,
   In passing by, but when she turns her face,
Thou must persist and seek her with desire,
   If thou wouldst win the favour of her grace.

And if, like some winged bird, she cleaves the air,
   And leaves thee spent and stricken on the earth,
Still must thou strive to follow even there,
   That she may know thy valour and thy worth.

Then shall she come unveiling all her charms,
   Giving thee joy for pain, and smiles for tears;
Then shalt thou clasp her with possessing arms,

The while she murmurs music in thine ears.

But ere her kiss has faded from thy cheek,
  She shall flee from thee over hill and glade,
So must thou seek and ever seek and seek
  For each new conquest of this phantom maid

THE WISH

Should some great angel say to me to-morrow,
  "Thou must re-tread thy pathway from the start,
But God will grant, in pity, for thy sorrow,
  Some one dear wish, the nearest to thy heart."

This were my wish!--from my life's dim beginning
  LET BE WHAT HAS BEEN! wisdom planned the whole
My want, my woe, my errors, and my sinning,
  All, all were needed lessons for my soul.

THREE FRIENDS

Of all the blessings which my life has known,
I value most, and most praise God for three:
Want, Loneliness, and Pain, those comrades true,

Who masqueraded in the garb of foes
For many a year, and filled my heart with dread.
Yet fickle joys, like false, pretentious friends,
Have proved less worthy than this trio. First,

Want taught me labour, led me up the steep
And toilsome paths to hills of pure delight,
Trod only by the feet that know fatigue,
And yet press on until the heights appear.

Then loneliness and hunger of the heart
Sent me upreaching to the realms of space,
Till all the silences grew eloquent,
And all their loving forces hailed me friend.

Last, pain taught prayer! placed in my hand the staff
Of close communion with the over-soul,
That I might lean upon it to the end,
And find myself made strong for any strife.

And then these three who had pursued my steps
Like stern, relentless foes, year after year,
Unmasked, and turned their faces full on me,
And lo! they were divinely beautiful,
For through them shone the lustrous eyes of Love.

YOU NEVER CAN TELL

You never can tell when you send a word,
  Like an arrow shot from a bow
By an archer blind, be it cruel or kind,
  Just where it may chance to go!
It may pierce the breast of your dearest friend,
  Tipped with its poison or balm;
To a stranger's heart in life's great mart,
  It may carry its pain or its calm.

You never can tell when you do an act
  Just what the result will be;
But with every deed you are sowing a seed,
  Though the harvest you may not see.
Each kindly act is an acorn dropped
  In God's productive soil.
You may not know, but the tree shall grow,
  With shelter for those who toil.

You never can tell what your thoughts will do,
  In bringing you hate or love;
For thoughts are things, and their airy wings
  Are swifter than carrier doves.
They follow the law of the universe -
  Each thing must create its kind;
And they speed o'er the track to bring you back
  WHATEVER WENT OUT FROM YOUR MIND.

HERE AND NOW

Here, in the heart of the world,
  Here, in the noise and the din,
Here, where our spirits were hurled
  To battle with sorrow and sin,
This is the place and the spot
  For knowledge of infinite things
This is the kingdom where Thought
  Can conquer the prowess of kings

Wait for no heavenly life,
  Seek for no temple alone;
Here, in the midst of the strife,
  Know what the sages have known.
See what the Perfect Ones saw -
  God in the depth of each soul,
God as the light and the law,
  God as beginning and goal.

Earth is one chamber of Heaven,
  Death is no grander than birth.
Joy in the life that was given,
  Strive for perfection on earth;
Here, in the turmoil and roar,
  Show what it is to be calm;
Show how the spirit can soar
  And bring hack its healing and balm.

Stand not aloof nor apart,
  Plunge in the thick of the fight;

There, in the street and the mart,
  That is the place to do right.
Not in some cloister or cave,
  Not in some kingdom above,
Here, on this side of the grave,
  Here, should we labour and love.

UNCONQUERED

However skilled and strong art thou, my foe,
However fierce is thy relentless hate,
Though firm thy hand, and strong thy aim, and straight
Thy poisoned arrow leaves the bended bow,

To pierce the target of my heart, ah! know
  I am the master yet of my own fate.
  Thou canst not rob me of my best estate,
Though fortune, fame, and friends, yea, love shall go.

Not to the dust shall my true self be hurled,
  Nor shall I meet thy worst assaults dismayed;
  When all things in the balance are well weighed,
There is but one great danger in the world -
  THOU CANST NOT FORCE MY SOUL TO WISH THEE ILL,
  That is the only evil that can kill.

ALL THAT LOVE ASKS

"All that I ask," says Love, "is just to stand
  And gaze, unchided, deep in thy dear eyes;
   For in their depths lies largest Paradise.
Yet, if perchance one pressure of thy hand
  Be granted me, then joy I thought complete
    Were still more sweet.

"All that I ask," says Love, "all that I ask,
  Is just thy hand-clasp. Could I brush thy cheek
   As zephyrs brush a rose leaf, words are weak
To tell the bliss in which my soul would bask.
  There is no language but would desecrate
    A joy so great.

"All that I ask, is just one tender touch
  Of that soft cheek. Thy pulsing palm in mine,
   Thy dark eyes lifted in a trust divine,
And those curled lips that tempt me overmuch
  Turned where I may not seize the supreme bliss
    Of one mad kiss.

"All that I ask," says Love, "of life, of death,
  Or of high heaven itself, is just to stand,
   Glance melting into glance, hand twined in hand,
The while I drink the nectar of thy breath
  In one sweet kiss, but one, of all thy store,
    I ask no more."

"All that I ask"--nay, self-deceiving Love,
Reverse thy phrase, so thus the words may fall,
In place of "all I ask," say, "I ask all,"
All that pertains to earth or soars above,
All that thou wert, art, will be, body, soul,
Love asks the whole,

"DOES IT PAY?"

If one poor burdened toiler o'er life's road,
Who meets us by the way,
Goes on less conscious of his galling load,
Then life, indeed, does pay.

If we can show one troubled heart the gain
That lies alway in loss,
Why, then, we too are paid for all the pain
Of bearing life's hard cross.

If some despondent soul to hope is stirred,
Some sad lip made to smile,
By any act of ours, or any word,
Then, life has been worth while.

SESTINA

I wandered o'er the vast green plains of youth,
And searched for Pleasure. On a distant height
Fame's silhouette stood sharp against the skies.
Beyond vast crowds that thronged a broad highway
I caught the glimmer of a golden goal,
While from a blooming bower smiled siren Love.

Straight gazing in her eyes, I laughed at Love
With all the haughty insolence of youth,
As past her bower I strode to seek my goal.
"Now will I climb to glory's dizzy height,"
I said, "for there above the common way
Doth pleasure dwell companioned by the skies."

But when I reached that summit near the skies,
So far from man I seemed, so far from Love -
"Not here," I cried, "doth Pleasure find her way."
Seen from the distant borderland of youth,
Fame smiles upon us from her sun-kissed height,
But frowns in shadows when we reach the goal.

Then were mine eyes fixed on that glittering goal,
Dear to all sense--sunk souls beneath the skies.
Gold tempts the artist from the lofty height,
Gold lures the maiden from the arms of Love,
Gold buys the fresh, ingenuous heart of youth,
"And gold," I said, "will show me Pleasure's way."

But ah! the soil and discord of that way,
Where savage hordes rushed headlong to the goal,
Dead to the best impulses of their youth,
Blind to the azure beauty of the skies;
Dulled to the voice of conscience and of love,
They wandered far from Truth's eternal height.

Then Truth spoke to me from that noble height,
Saying, "Thou didst pass Pleasure on the way,
She with the yearning eyes so full of Love,
Whom thou disdained to seek for glory's goal.
Two blending paths beneath God's arching skies
Lead straight to Pleasure. Ah! blind heart of youth,
Not up fame's height, not toward the base god's goal,
Doth Pleasure make her way, but 'neath calm skies
Where Duty walks with Love in endless youth."

THE OPTIMIST

The fields were bleak and sodden.
    Not a wing
Or note enlivened the depressing wood;
A soiled and sullen, stubborn snowdrift stood
Beside the roadway. Winds came muttering
Of storms to be, and brought the chilly sting
    Of icebergs in their breath. Stalled cattle mooed
    Forth plaintive pleadings for the earth's green food.
No gleam, no hint of hope in anything.

The sky was blank and ashen, like the face
  Of some poor wretch who drains life's cup too fast
Yet, swaying to and fro, as if to fling
About chilled Nature its lithe arms of grace,
  Smiling with promise in the wintry blast,
The optimistic Willow spoke of spring.

THE PESSIMIST

The pessimistic locust, last to leaf,
Though all the world is glad, still talks of grief.

AN INSPIRATION

However the battle is ended,
  Though proudly the victor comes
With fluttering flags and prancing nags
  And echoing roll of drums,
Still truth proclaims this motto
  In letters of living light, -
No question is ever settled
  Until it is settled right.

Though the heel of the strong oppressor
  May grind the weak in the dust;
And the voices of fame with one acclaim

May call him great and just,
Let those who applaud take warning.
  And keep this motto in sight, -
No question is ever settled
  Until it is settled right.

Let those who have failed take courage;
  Though the enemy seems to have won,
Though his ranks are strong, if he be in the wrong
  The battle is not yet done;
For, sure as the morning follows
  The darkest hour of the night,
No question is ever settled
  Until it is settled right.

O man bowed down with labour!
  O woman young, yet old!
O heart oppressed in the toiler's breast
  And crushed by the power of gold
Keep on with your weary battle
  Against triumphant might;
No question is ever settled
  Until it is settled right.

LIFE'S HARMONIES

Let no man pray that he know not sorrow,
   Let no soul ask to be free from pain,
For the gall of to-day is the sweet of to-morrow,
   And the moment's loss is the lifetime's gain.

Through want of a thing does its worth redouble,
   Through hunger's pangs does the feast content,
And only the heart that has harboured trouble
   Can fully rejoice when joy is sent.

Let no man shrink from the bitter tonics
   Of grief, and yearning, and need, and strife,
For the rarest chords in the soul's harmonics
   Are found in the minor strains of life.

PREPARATION

We must not force events, but rather make
The heart soil ready for their coming, as
The earth spreads carpets for the feet of Spring,
Or, with the strengthening tonic of the frost,
Prepares for winter. Should a July noon
Burst suddenly upon a frozen world
Small joy would follow, even though that world
Were longing for the Summer. Should the sting

Of sharp December pierce the heart of June,
What death and devastation would ensue!
All things are planned. The most majestic sphere
That whirls through space is governed and controlled
By supreme law, as is the blade of grass
Which through the bursting bosom of the earth
Creeps up to kiss the light. Poor, puny man
Alone doth strive and battle with the Force
Which rules all lives and worlds, and he alone
Demands effect before producing cause.
How vain the hope! We cannot harvest joy
Until we sow the seed, and God alone
Knows when that seed has ripened. Oft we stand
And watch the ground with anxious, brooding eyes,
Complaining of the slow, unfruitful yield,
Not knowing that the shadow of ourselves
Keeps off the sunlight and delays result.
Sometimes our fierce impatience of desire
Doth like a sultry May force tender shoots
Of half-formed pleasures and unshaped events
To ripen prematurely, and we reap
But disappointment; or we rot the germs
With briny tears ere they have time to grow.
While stars are born and mighty planets die
And hissing comets scorch the brow of space,
The Universe keeps its eternal calm.
Through patient preparation, year on year,
The earth endures the travail of the Spring
And Winter's desolation. So our souls
In grand submission to a higher law
Should move serene through all the ills of life
Believing them masked joys.

GETHSEMANE

In golden youth when seems the earth
A Summer-land of singing mirth,
When souls are glad and hearts are light,
And not a shadow lurks in sight,
We do not know it, but there lieu
Somewhere veiled under evening skies
A garden which we all must see -
The garden of Gethsemane.

With joyous steps we go our ways,
Love lends a halo to our days;
Light sorrows sail like clouds afar,
We laugh, and say how strong we are.
We hurry on; and hurrying, go
Close to the borderland of woe
That waits for you, and waits for me -
Forever waits Gethsemane.

Down shadowy lanes, across strange streams,
Bridged over by our broken dreams;
Behind the misty caps of years,
Beyond the great salt fount of tears,
The garden lies. Strive as you may,
You cannot miss it in your way;
All paths that have been, or shall be,
Pass somewhere through Gethsemane.

All those who journey, soon or late,
Must pass within the garden's gate;

Must kneel alone in darkness there,
And battle with some fierce despair.
God pity those who cannot say,
"Not mine but Thine"; who only pray
"Let this cup pass," and cannot see
The PURPOSE in Gethsemane.

GOD'S MEASURE

God measures souls by their capacity
For entertaining his best Angel, Love.
Who loveth most is nearest kin to God,
Who is all Love, or Nothing.

    He who sits
And looks out on the palpitating world,
And feels his heart swell in him large enough
To hold all men within it, he is near
His great Creator's standard, though he dwells
Outside the pale of churches, and knows not
A feast-day from a fast-day, or a line
Of Scripture even. What God wants of us
Is that outreaching bigness that ignores
All littleness of aims, or loves, or creeds,
And clasps all Earth and Heaven in its embrace.

NOBLESSE OBLIGE

I hold it the duty of one who is gifted
   And specially dowered in all men's sight,
To know no rest till his life is lifted
   Fully up to his great gifts' height.

He must mould the man into rare completeness,
   For gems are set only in gold refined.
He must fashion his thoughts into perfect sweetness.
   And cast out folly and pride from his mind.

For he who drinks from a god's gold fountain
   Of art or music or rhythmic song
Must sift from his soul the chaff of malice,
   And weed from his heart the roots of wrong.

Great gifts should be worn, like a crown befitting,
   And not like gems in a beggar's hands!
And the toil must be constant and unremitting
   Which lifts up the king to the crown's demands.

THROUGH TEARS

An artist toiled over his pictures;
  He laboured by night and by day,
He struggled for glory and honour
  But the world, it had nothing to say.
His walls were ablaze with the splendours
  We see in the beautiful skies;
But the world beheld only the colours
  That were made out of chemical dyes.

Time sped. And he lived, loved, and suffered;
  He passed through the valley of grief.
Again he toiled over his canvas,
  Since in labour alone was relief.
It showed not the splendour of colours
  Of those of his earlier years;
But the world? the world bowed down before it
  Because it was painted with tears.

A poet was gifted with genius,
  And he sang, and he sang all the days.
He wrote for the praise of the people,
  But the people accorded no praise.
Oh! his songs were as blithe as the morning,
  As sweet as the music of birds;
But the world had no homage to offer,
  Because they were nothing but words.

Time sped. And the poet through sorrow
  Became like his suffering kind.

Again he toiled over his poems
　To lighten the grief of his mind.
They were not so flowing and rhythmic
　As those of his earlier years;
But the world? lo! it offered its homage,
　Because they were written in tears.

So ever the price must be given
　By those seeking glory in art;
So ever the world is repaying
　The grief-stricken, suffering heart.
The happy must ever be humble;
　Ambition must wait for the years
Ere hoping to win the approval
　Of a world that looks on through its tears.

WHAT WE NEED

What does our country need? No armies standing
　With sabres gleaming ready for the fight;
Not increased navies, skilful and commanding,
　To bound the waters with an iron might;
Not haughty men with glutted purses trying
　To purchase souls, and keep the power of place;
Not jewelled dolls with one another vying
　For palms of beauty, elegance, and grace.

But we want women, strong of soul, yet lowly,
　With that rare meekness, born of gentleness;
Women whose lives are pure and clean and holy,

The women whom all little children bless;
Brave, earnest women, helpful to each other,
   With finest scorn for all things low and mean;
Women who hold the names of wife and mother
   Far nobler than the title of a queen.

Oh! these are they who mould the men of story,
   These mothers, ofttimes shorn of grace and youth,
Who, worn and weary, ask no greater glory
   Than making some young soul the home of truth;
Who sow in hearts all fallow for the sowing
   The seeds of virtue and of scorn for sin,
And, patient, watch the beauteous harvest growing
   And weed out tares which crafty hands cast in;

Women who do not hold the gift of beauty
   As some rare treasure to be bought and sold.
But guard it as a precious aid to duty -
   The outer framing of the inner gold;
Women who, low above their cradles bending,
   Let flattery's voice go by, and give no heed,
While their pure prayers like incense are ascending
   THESE are our country's pride, our country's need,

PLEA TO SCIENCE

O Science, reaching backward through the distance,
　　Most earnest child of God,
Exposing all the secrets of existence,
　　With thy divining rod,
I bid thee speed up to the heights supernal,
　　Clear thinker, ne'er sufficed;
Go seek and bind the laws and truths eternal,
　　But leave me Christ.

Upon the vanity of pious sages
　　Let in the light of day;
Break down the superstitions of all ages -
　　Thrust bigotry away;
Stride on, and bid all stubborn foes defiance,
　　Let Truth and Reason reign:
But I beseech thee, O Immortal Science,
　　Let Christ remain.

What canst thou give to help me bear my crosses,
　　In place of Him, my Lord?
And what to recompense for all my losses,
　　And bring me sweet reward?
THOU couldst not with thy clear, cold eyes of reason,
　　Thou couldst not comfort me
Like One who passed through that tear-blotted season
　　In sad Gethsemane!

Through all the weary, wearing hour of sorrow,
　　What word that thou hast said

Would make me strong to wait for some to-morrow
  When I should find my dead?
When I am weak, and desolate, and lonely -
  And prone to follow wrong?
Not thou, O Science--Christ, my Saviour, only
  Can make me strong.

Thou art so cold, so lofty, and so distant,
  Though great my need might be,
No prayer, however constant and persistent,
  Could bring thee down to me.
Christ stands so near, to help me through each hour,
  To guide me day by day
O Science, sweeping all before thy power -
  Leave Christ, I pray!

RESPITE

The mighty conflict, which we call existence,
  Doth wear upon the body and the soul,
Our vital forces wasted in resistance,
  So much there is to conquer and control.

The rock which meets the billows with defiance,
  Undaunted and unshaken day by day,
In spite of its unyielding self-reliance,
  Is by the warfare surely worn away.

And there are depths and heights of strong emotions
  That surge at times within the human breast,

More fierce than all the tides of all the oceans
  Which sweep on ever in divine unrest.

I sometimes think the rock worn with adventures,
  And sad with thoughts of conflicts yet to be,
Must envy the frail reed which no one censures,
  When, overcome, 'tis swallowed by the sea.

This life is all resistance and repression.
  Dear God, if in that other world unseen,
Not rest we find, but new life and progression,
  Grant us a respite in the grave between.

SONG

O praise me not with your lips, dear one!
  Though your tender words I prize.
But dearer by far is the soulful gaze
  Of your eyes, your beautiful eyes
    Your tender, loving eyes.

O chide me not with your lips, dear one!
  Though I cause your bosom sighs.
You can make repentance deeper far
  By your sad, reproving eyes,
    Your sorrowful, troubled eyes.

Words, at the best, are but hollow sounds;
  Above, in the beaming skies,
The constant stars say never a word,

But only smile with their eyes -
　Smile on with their lustrous eyes.

Then breathe no vow with your lips, dear one;
　On the winged wind speech flies.
But I read the truth of your noble heart
　In your soulful, speaking eyes -
　　In your deep and beautiful eyes.

MY SHIPS

If all the ships I have at sea
Should come a-sailing home to me,
Ah, well! the harbour could not hold
So many sails as there would be
If all my ships came in from sea.

If half my ships came home from sea,
And brought their precious freight to me,
Ah, well! I should have wealth as great
As any king who sits in state -
So rich the treasures that would be
In half my ships now out at sea.

If just one ship I have at sea
Should come a-sailing home to me,
Ah, well! the storm-clouds then might frown
For if the others all went down,
Still rich and proud and glad I'd be
If that one ship came back to me.

If that one ship went down at sea,
And all the others came to me,
Weighed down with gems and wealth untold,
With glory, honours, riches, gold,
The poorest soul on earth I'd be
If that one ship came not to me.

O skies, be calm! O winds, blow free -
Blow all my ships safe home to me!
But if thou sendest some a-wrack,
To never more come sailing back,
Send any--all that skim the sea,
But bring my love-ship home to me.

HER LOVE

The sands upon the ocean side
That change about with every tide,
And never true to one abide,
  A woman's love I liken to.

The summer zephyrs, light and vain,
That sing the same alluring strain
To every grass blade on the plain -
  A woman's love is nothing more.

The sunshine of an April day
That comes to warm you with its ray,
But while you smile has flown away -
  A woman's love is like to this.

God made poor woman with no heart,
But gave her skill, and tact, and art,
And so she lives, and plays her part.
   We must not blame, but pity her.

She leans to man--but just to hear
The praise he whispers in her ear;
Herself, not him, she holdeth dear -
   O fool! to be deceived by her.

To sate her selfish thirst she quaffs
The love of strong hearts in sweet draughts,
Then throws them lightly by and laughs,
   Too weak to understand their pain.

As changeful as the winds that blow
From every region to and fro,
Devoid of heart, she cannot know
   The suffering of a human heart.

IF

Dear love, if you and I could sail away,
  With snowy pennons to the winds unfurled,
Across the waters of some unknown bay,
  And find some island far from all the world;

If we could dwell there, evermore alone,
  While unrecorded years slip by apace,
Forgetting and forgotten and unknown
  By aught save native song-birds of the place;

If Winter never visited that land,
  And Summer's lap spilled o'er with fruits and flowers,
And tropic trees cast shade on every hand,
  And twined boughs formed sleep-inviting bowers;

If from the fashions of the world set free,
  And hid away from all its jealous strife,
I lived alone for you, and you for me -
  Ah! then, dear love, how sweet were wedded life.

But since we dwell here in the crowded way,
  Where hurrying throngs rush by to seek for gold,
And all is commonplace and work-a-day
  As soon as love's young honeymoon grows old;

Since fashion rules and nature yields to art,
  And life is hurt by daily jar and fret,
'Tis best to shut such dreams down in the heart
  And go our ways alone, love, and forget.

LOVE'S BURIAL

Let us clear a little space,
And make Love a burial-place.

He is dead, dear, as you see,
And he wearies you and me.

Growing heavier, day by day,
Let us bury him, I say.

Wings of dead white butterflies,
These shall shroud him, as he lies

In his casket rich and rare,
Made of finest maiden-hair.

With the pollen of the rose
Let us his white eyelids close.

Put the rose thorn in his hand,
Shorn of leaves--you understand.

Let some holy water fall
On his dead face, tears of gall -

As we kneel to him and say,
"Dreams to dreams," and turn away.

Those gravediggers, Doubt, Distrust,
They will lower him to the dust.

Let us part here with a kiss -
You go that way, I go this.

Since we buried Love to-day
We will walk a separate way.

"LOVE IS ENOUGH"

Love is enough. Let us not ask for gold.
   Wealth breeds false aims, and pride, and selfishness;
In those serene, Arcadian days of old
   Men gave no thought to princely homes and dress.
The gods who dwelt on fair Olympia's height
Lived only for dear love and love's delight.
    Love is enough.

Love is enough. Why should we care for fame?
   Ambition is a most unpleasant guest:
It lures us with the glory of a name
   Far from the happy haunts of peace and rest.
Let us stay here in this secluded place
Made beautiful by love's endearing grace!
    Love is enough.

Love is enough. Why should we strive for power?
   It brings men only envy and distrust.
The poor world's homage pleases but an hour,
   And earthly honours vanish in the dust.
The grandest lives are ofttimes desolate;

Let me be loved, and let who will be great.
   Love is enough.

Love is enough. Why should we ask for more?
  What greater gift have gods vouchsafed to men?
What better boon of all their precious store
  Than our fond hearts that love and love again?
Old love may die; new love is just as sweet;
And life is fair and all the world complete:
   Love is enough!

LIFE IS A PRIVILEGE

Life is a privilege. Its youthful days
Shine with the radiance of continuous Mays.
To live, to breathe, to wonder and desire,
To feed with dreams the heart's perpetual fire,
To thrill with virtuous passions, and to glow
With great ambitions--in one hour to know
The depths and heights of feeling--God! in truth,
How beautiful, how beautiful is youth!

Life is a privilege. Like some rare rose
The mysteries of the human mind unclose.
What marvels lie in earth, and air, and sea!
What stores of knowledge wait our opening key!
What sunny roads of happiness lead out
Beyond the realms of indolence and doubt!
And what large pleasures smile upon and bless
The busy avenues of usefulness!

Life is a privilege. Though noontide fades
And shadows fall along the winding glades,
Though joy-blooms wither in the autumn air,
Yet the sweet scent of sympathy is there.
Pale sorrow leads us closer to our kind,
And in the serious hours of life we find
Depths in the souls of men which lend new worth
And majesty to this brief span of earth.

Life is a privilege. If some sad fate
Sends us alone to seek the exit gate,
If men forsake us and as shadows fall,
Still does the supreme privilege of all
Come in that reaching upward of the soul
To find the welcoming Presence at the goal,
And in the Knowledge that our feet have trod
Paths that led from, and must wind back, to God.

INSIGHT

Sirs, when you pity us, I say
You waste your pity. Let it stay,
Well corked and stored upon your shelves,
Until you need it for yourselves.

We do appreciate God's thought
In forming you, before He brought
Us into life. His art was crude,
But oh! so virile in its rude,

Large, elemental strength; and then
He learned His trade in making men,
Learned how to mix and mould the clay
And fashion in a finer way.

How fine that skilful way can be
You need but lift your eyes to see;
And we are glad God placed you there
To lift your eyes and find us fair.

Apprentice labour though you were,
He made you great enough to stir
The best and deepest depths of us,
And we are glad He made you thus.

Aye! we are glad of many things;
God strung our hearts with such fine strings
The least breath moves them, and we hear
Music where silence greets your ear.

We suffer so? But women's souls,
Like violet-powder dropped on coals,
Give forth their best in anguish. Oh
The subtle secrets that we know

Of joy in sorrow, strange delights
Of ecstasy in pain-filled nights,
And mysteries of gain in loss
Known but to Christ upon the cross!

Our tears are pitiful to you?
Look how the heaven-reflecting dew
Dissolves its life in tears. The sand

Meanwhile lies hard upon the strand.

How could your pity find a place
For us, the mothers of the race?
Men may be fathers unaware,
So poor the title is you wear.

But mothers--who that crown adorns
Knows all its mingled blooms and thorns,
And she whose feet that pain hath trod
Hath walked upon the heights with God.

No, offer us not pity's cup.
There is no looking down or up
Between us; eye looks straight in eye:
Born equals, so we live and die.

A WOMAN'S ANSWER

You call me an angel of love and of light,
    A being of goodness and heavenly fire,
Sent out from God's kingdom to guide you aright,
    In paths where your spirit may mount and aspire,
You say that I glow like a star on its course,
Like a ray from the altar, a spark from the source.

Now list to my answer--let all the world hear it,
    I speak unafraid what I know to be true -
A pure, faithful love is the creative spirit
    Which make women angels! I live but in you.

We are bound soul to soul by life's holiest laws;
If I am an angel--why, you are the cause.

As my ship skims the sea, I look up from the deck.
   Fair, firm at the wheel shines Love's beautiful form.
And shall I curse the bark that last night went to wreck
   By the pilot abandoned to darkness and storm?
My craft is no stauncher, she too had been lost
Had the wheelman deserted, or slept at his post.

I laid down the wealth of my soul at your feet
   (Some woman does this for some man every day).
No desperate creature who walks in the street
   Has a wickeder heart than I might have, I say,
Had you wantonly misused the treasures you won -
As so many men with heart-riches have done.

This fire from God's altar, this holy love-flame,
   That burns like sweet incense forever for you,
Might now be a wild conflagration of shame,
   Had you tortured my heart, or been base or untrue.
For angels and devils are cast in one mould,
Till love guides them upward or downward, I hold.

I tell you the women who make fervent wives
   And sweet tender mothers, had Fate been less fair,
Are the women who might have abandoned their lives
   To the madness that springs from and ends in despair.
As the fire on the hearth which sheds brightness around,
Neglected, may level the walls to the ground.

The world makes grave errors in judging these things.
   Great good and great evil are born in one breast:

Love horns us and hoofs us, or gives us our wings,
   And the best could be worst, as the worst could be best.
You must thank your own worth for what I grew to be,
For the demon lurked under the angel in me.

THE WORLD'S NEED

So many gods, so many creeds,
   So many paths that wind and wind,
   While just the art of being kind,
Is all the sad world needs.

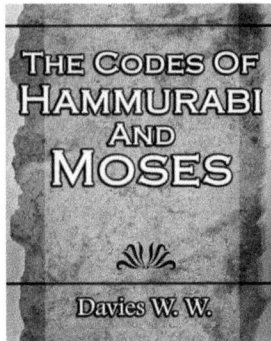

The Codes Of Hammurabi And Moses
W. W. Davies

QTY

The discovery of the Hammurabi Code is one of the greatest achievements of archaeology, and is of paramount interest, not only to the student of the Bible, but also to all those interested in ancient history...

Religion   **ISBN:** *1-59462-338-4*   **Pages:132**
                                                     MSRP $12.95

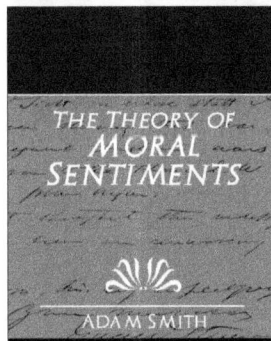

The Theory of Moral Sentiments
Adam Smith

QTY

This work from 1749. contains original theories of conscience amd moral judgment and it is the foundation for systemof morals.

Philosophy   **ISBN:** *1-59462-777-0*   **Pages:536**
                                                     MSRP $19.95

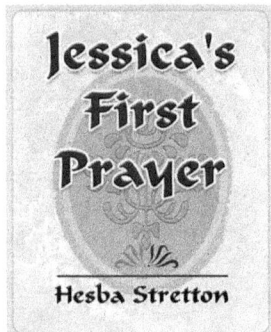

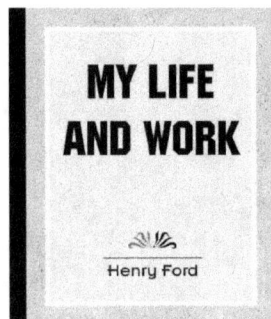

Jessica's First Prayer
Hesba Stretton

QTY

In a screened and secluded corner of one of the many railway-bridges which span the streets of London there could be seen a few years ago, from five o'clock every morning until half past eight, a tidily set-out coffee-stall, consisting of a trestle and board, upon which stood two large tin cans, with a small fire of charcoal burning under each so as to keep the coffee boiling during the early hours of the morning when the work-people were thronging into the city on their way to their daily toil...

Pages:84

Childrens   **ISBN:** *1-59462-373-2*   *MSRP $9.95*

My Life and Work
Henry Ford

QTY

Henry Ford revolutionized the world with his implementation of mass production for the Model T automobile. Gain valuable business insight into his life and work with his own auto-biography... "We have only started on our development of our country we have not as yet, with all our talk of wonderful progress, done more than scratch the surface. The progress has been wonderful enough but..."

Pages:300

Biographies/   **ISBN:** *1-59462-198-5*   *MSRP $21.95*

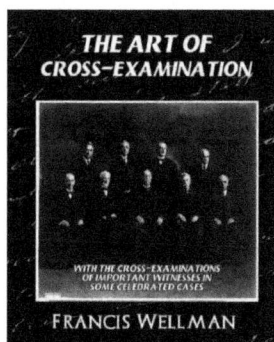

The Art of Cross-Examination
Francis Wellman

QTY

I presume it is the experience of every author, after his first book is published upon an important subject, to be almost overwhelmed with a wealth of ideas and illustrations which could readily have been included in his book, and which to his own mind, at least, seem to make a second edition inevitable. Such certainly was the case with me; and when the first edition had reached its sixth impression in five months, I rejoiced to learn that it seemed to my publishers that the book had met with a sufficiently favorable reception to justify a second and considerably enlarged edition. ..

Pages:412

Reference   **ISBN:** *1-59462-647-2*   *MSRP $19.95*

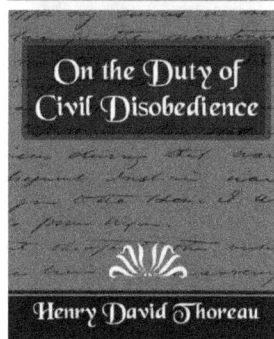

On the Duty of Civil Disobedience
Henry David Thoreau

QTY

Thoreau wrote his famous essay, On the Duty of Civil Disobedience, as a protest against an unjust but popular war and the immoral but popular institution of slave-owning. He did more than write—he declined to pay his taxes, and was hauled off to gaol in consequence. Who can say how much this refusal of his hastened the end of the war and of slavery ?

Law   **ISBN:** *1-59462-747-9*   **Pages:48**

MSRP $7.45

Dream Psychology Psychoanalysis for Beginners
Sigmund Freud

QTY

Sigmund Freud, born Sigismund Schlomo Freud (May 6, 1856 - September 23, 1939), was a Jewish-Austrian neurologist and psychiatrist who co-founded the psychoanalytic school of psychology. Freud is best known for his theories of the unconscious mind, especially involving the mechanism of repression; his redefinition of sexual desire as mobile and directed towards a wide variety of objects; and his therapeutic techniques, especially his understanding of transference in the therapeutic relationship and the presumed value of dreams as sources of insight into unconscious desires.

Pages:196

Psychology   **ISBN:** *1-59462-905-6*   *MSRP $15.45*

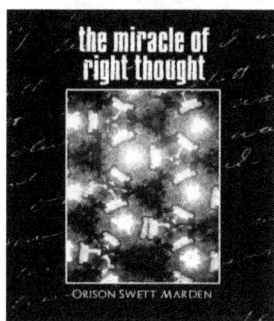

The Miracle of Right Thought
Orison Swett Marden

QTY

Believe with all of your heart that you will do what you were made to do. When the mind has once formed the habit of holding cheerful, happy, prosperous pictures, it will not be easy to form the opposite habit. It does not matter how improbable or how far away this realization may see, or how dark the prospects may be, if we visualize them as best we can, as vividly as possible, hold tenaciously to them and vigorously struggle to attain them, they will gradually become actualized, realized in the life. But a desire, a longing without endeavor, a yearning abandoned or held indifferently will vanish without realization.

Pages:360

Self Help   **ISBN:** *1-59462-644-8*   *MSRP $25.45*

www.bookjungle.com *email: sales@bookjungle.com fax: 630-214-0564 mail: Book Jungle PO Box 2226 Champaign, IL 61825*

QTY

The Rosicrucian Cosmo-Conception Mystic Christianity *by Max Heindel*　ISBN: *1-59462-188-8*　**$38.95**
The Rosicrucian Cosmo-conception is not dogmatic, neither does it appeal to any other authority than the reason of the student. It is: not controversial, but is: sent forth in the, hope that it may help to clear..　New Age/Religion Pages 646

Abandonment To Divine Providence *by Jean-Pierre de Caussade*　ISBN: *1-59462-228-0*　**$25.95**
"The Rev. Jean Pierre de Caussade was one of the most remarkable spiritual writers of the Society of Jesus in France in the 18th Century. His death took place at Toulouse in 1751. His works have gone through many editions and have been republished...　Inspirational/Religion Pages 400

Mental Chemistry *by Charles Haanel*　ISBN: *1-59462-192-6*　**$23.95**
Mental Chemistry allows the change of material conditions by combining and appropriately utilizing the power of the mind. Much like applied chemistry creates something new and unique out of careful combinations of chemicals the mastery of mental chemistry...　New Age Pages 354

The Letters of Robert Browning and Elizabeth Barret Barrett 1845-1846 vol II　ISBN: *1-59462-193-4*　**$35.95**
by Robert Browning and *Elizabeth Barrett*　Biographies Pages 596

Gleanings In Genesis (volume I) *by Arthur W. Pink*　ISBN: *1-59462-130-6*　**$27.45**
Appropriately has Genesis been termed "the seed plot of the Bible" for in it we have, in germ form, almost all of the great doctrines which are afterwards fully developed in the books of Scripture which follow...　Religion/Inspirational Pages 420

The Master Key *by L. W. de Laurence*　ISBN: *1-59462-001-6*　**$30.95**
In no branch of human knowledge has there been a more lively increase of the spirit of research during the past few years than in the study of Psychology, Concentration and Mental Discipline. The requests for authentic lessons in Thought Control, Mental Discipline and...　New Age/Business Pages 422

The Lesser Key Of Solomon Goetia *by L. W. de Laurence*　ISBN: *1-59462-092-X*　**$9.95**
This translation of the first book of the "Lemegton" which is now for the first time made accessible to students of Talismanic Magic was done, after careful collation and edition, from numerous Ancient Manuscripts in Hebrew, Latin, and French...　New Age/Occult Pages 92

Rubaiyat Of Omar Khayyam *by Edward Fitzgerald*　ISDN:*1-59462-332-5*　**$13.95**
Edward Fitzgerald, whom the world has already learned, in spite of his own efforts to remain within the shadow of anonymity, to look upon as one of the rarest poets of the century, was born at Bredfield, in Suffolk, on the 31st of March, 1809. He was the third son of John Purcell...　Music Pages 172

Ancient Law *by Henry Maine*　ISBN: *1-59462-128-4*　**$29.95**
The chief object of the following pages is to indicate some of the earliest ideas of mankind, as they are reflected in Ancient Law, and to point out the relation of those ideas to modern thought.　Religion/History Pages 452

Far-Away Stories *by William J. Locke*　ISBN: *1-59462-129-2*　**$19.45**
"Good wine needs no bush, but a collection of mixed vintages does. And this book is just such a collection. Some of the stories I do not want to remain buried for ever in the museum files of dead magazine-numbers an author's not unpardonable vanity..."　Fiction Pages 272

Life of David Crockett *by David Crockett*　ISBN: *1-59462-250-7*　**$27.45**
"Colonel David Crockett was one of the most remarkable men of the times in which he lived. Born in humble life, but gifted with a strong will, an indomitable courage, and unremitting perseverance...　Biographies/New Age Pages 424

Lip-Reading *by Edward Nitchie*　ISBN: *1-59462-206-X*　**$25.95**
Edward B. Nitchie, founder of the New York School for the Hard of Hearing, now the Nitchie School of Lip-Reading, Inc, wrote "LIP-READING Principles and Practice". The development and perfecting of this meritorious work on lip-reading was an undertaking...　How-to Pages 400

A Handbook of Suggestive Therapeutics, Applied Hypnotism, Psychic Science　ISBN: *1-59462-214-0*　**$24.95**
by Henry Munro　Health/New Age/Health/Self-help Pages 376

A Doll's House: and Two Other Plays *by Henrik Ibsen*　ISBN: *1-59462-112-8*　**$19.95**
Henrik Ibsen created this classic when in revolutionary 1848 Rome. Introducing some striking concepts in playwriting for the realist genre, this play has been studied the world over.　Fiction/Classics/Plays 308

The Light of Asia *by sir Edwin Arnold*　ISBN: *1-59462-204-3*　**$13.95**
In this poetic masterpiece, Edwin Arnold describes the life and teachings of Buddha. The man who was to become known as Buddha to the world was born as Prince Gautama of India but he rejected the worldly riches and abandoned the reigns of power when...　Religion/History/Biographies Pages 170

The Complete Works of Guy de Maupassant *by Guy de Maupassant*　ISBN: *1-59462-157-8*　**$16.95**
"For days and days, nights and nights, I had dreamed of that first kiss which was to consecrate our engagement, and I knew not on what spot I should put my lips..."　Fiction/Classics Pages 240

The Art of Cross-Examination *by Francis L. Wellman*　ISBN: *1-59462-309-0*　**$26.95**
Written by a renowned trial lawyer, Wellman imparts his experience and uses case studies to explain how to use psychology to extract desired information through questioning.　How-to/Science/Reference Pages 408

Answered or Unanswered? *by Louisa Vaughan*　ISBN: *1-59462-248-5*　**$10.95**
Miracles of Faith in China　Religion Pages 112

The Edinburgh Lectures on Mental Science (1909) *by Thomas*　ISBN: *1-59462-008-3*　**$11.95**
This book contains the substance of a course of lectures recently given by the writer in the Queen Street Hall, Edinburgh. Its purpose is to indicate the Natural Principles governing the relation between Mental Action and Material Conditions...　New Age/Psychology Pages 148

Ayesha *by H. Rider Haggard*　ISBN: *1-59462-301-5*　**$24.95**
Verily and indeed it is the unexpected that happens! Probably if there was one person upon the earth from whom the Editor of this, and of a certain previous history, did not expect to hear again...　Classics Pages 380

Ayala's Angel *by Anthony Trollope*　ISBN: *1-59462-352-X*　**$29.95**
The two girls were both pretty, but Lucy who was twenty-one who supposed to be simple and comparatively unattractive, whereas Ayala was credited, as her Bombwhat romantic name might show, with poetic charm and a taste for romance. Ayala when her father died was nineteen...　Fiction Pages 484

The American Commonwealth *by James Bryce*　ISBN: *1-59462-286-8*　**$34.45**
An interpretation of American democratic political theory. It examines political mechanics and society from the perspective of Scotsman James Bryce　Politics Pages 572

Stories of the Pilgrims *by Margaret P. Pumphrey*　ISBN: *1-59462-116-0*　**$17.95**
This book explores pilgrims religious oppression in England as well as their escape to Holland and eventual crossing to America on the Mayflower, and their early days in New England...　History Pages 268

QTY

The Fasting Cure *by **Sinclair Upton***   ISBN: *1-59462-222-1*   **$13.95**
*In the Cosmopolitan Magazine for May, 1910, and in the Contemporary Review (London) for April, 1910, I published an article dealing with my experi-
ences in fasting. I have written a great many magazine articles, but never one which attracted so much attention...*   New Age/Self Help/Health Pages 164

Hebrew Astrology *by **Sepharial***   ISBN: *1-59462-308-2*   **$13.45**
*In these days of advanced thinking it is a matter of common observation that we have left many of the old landmarks behind and that we are now pressing
forward to greater heights and to a wider horizon than that which represented the mind-content of our progenitors...*   Astrology Pages 144

Thought Vibration or The Law of Attraction in the Thought World   ISBN: *1-59462-127-6*   **$12.95**

*by **William Walker Atkinson***   Psychology/Religion Pages 144

Optimism *by **Helen Keller***   ISBN: *1-59462-108-X*   **$15.95**
*Helen Keller was blind, deaf, and mute since 19 months old, yet famously learned how to overcome these handicaps, communicate with the world, and
spread her lectures promoting optimism. An inspiring read for everyone...*   Biographies/Inspirational Pages 84

Sara Crewe *by **Frances Burnett***   ISBN: *1-59462-360-0*   **$9.45**
*In the first place, Miss Minchin lived in London. Her home was a large, dull, tall one, in a large, dull square, where all the houses were alike, and all the
sparrows were alike, and where all the door-knockers made the same heavy sound...*   Childrens/Classic Pages 88

The Autobiography of Benjamin Franklin *by **Benjamin Franklin***   ISBN: *1-59462-135-7*   **$24.95**
*The Autobiography of Benjamin Franklin has probably been more extensively read than any other American historical work, and no other book of its kind
has had such ups and downs of fortune. Franklin lived for many years in England, where he was agent...*   Biographies/History Pages 332

Name	
Email	
Telephone	
Address	
City, State ZIP	

☐ **Credit Card**   ☐ **Check / Money Order**

Credit Card Number	
Expiration Date	
Signature	

Please Mail to: Book Jungle
PO Box 2226
Champaign, IL 61825
or Fax to: 630-214-0564

ORDERING INFORMATION

web*: www.bookjungle.com*
email*: sales@bookjungle.com*
fax*: 630-214-0564*
mail*: Book Jungle PO Box 2226 Champaign, IL 61825*
or PayPal *to sales@bookjungle.com*

Please contact us for bulk discounts

DIRECT-ORDER TERMS

**20% Discount if You Order
Two or More Books**
Free Domestic Shipping!
Accepted: Master Card, Visa,
Discover, American Express

www.ingramcontent.com/pod-product-compliance
Lightning Source LLC
LaVergne TN
LVHW081324060426
835511LV00011B/1841